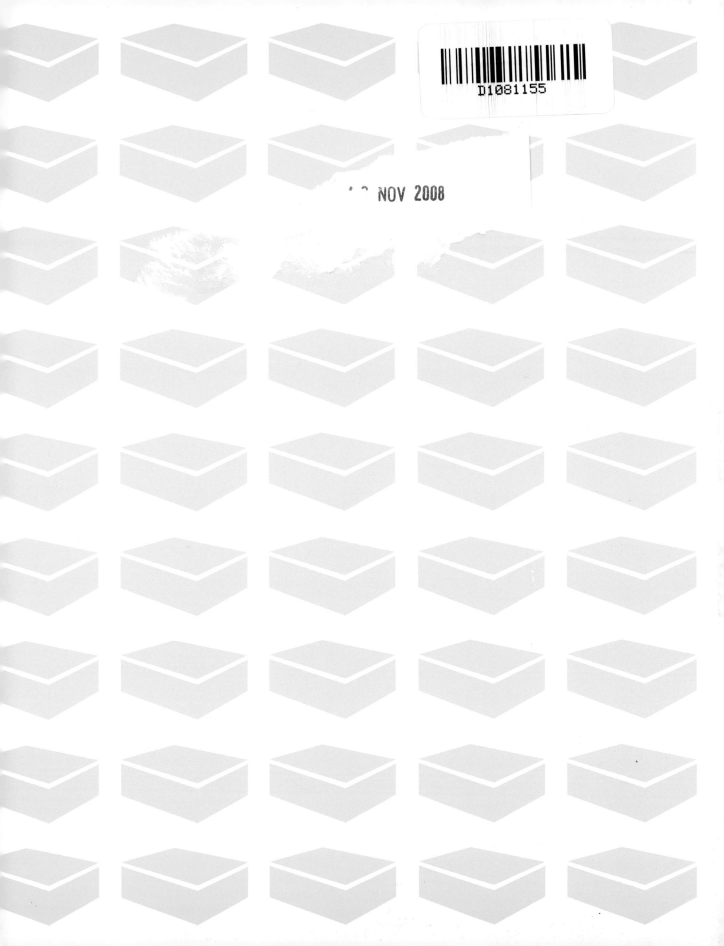

Packaging

Lynn Huggins-Cooper

A & C Black • London

Published 2007 by A & C Black Publishers Limited
38 Soho Square, London W1D 3HB
www.acblack.com

Hardback ISBN: 978-0-7136-7111-7
Paperback ISBN: 978-0-7136-7685-3

Editor: Sarah Gay
Designer: Miranda Snow

The author and publishers would like to thank Clare Benson and Sue Dutson for their advice in producing this series of books.

A CIP catalogue record for this book is available from the British Library.

This book is produced using paper that is made from wood grown in managed, sustainable forests. It is natural, renewable and recyclable. The logging and manufacturing processes conform to the environmental regulations of the country of origin.

Printed and bound in Singapore by Tien Wah Press (PTE) Limited.

Picture credits: front cover(br), Dianne Maire/Shutterstock; back cover, Stephen Coburn/Shutterstock; 4, Robert Harding Picture Library Ltd/Alamy; 5, Jack Sullivan/Alamy; 6, PEMCO-Webster & Stevens Collection; Museum of History and Industry, Seattle/Corbis; 7, Danita Delimont/Alamy; 8(tl), image100/Corbis; 8(tr), Lew Robinson/Getty Images; 8(bl), Tin Roof Images/Alamy; 8(br), Rolf Richardson/Alamy; 9(tl), BananaStock/Alamy; 9(tr), Photomax/Alamy; 9(bl), Jeff Greenberg/Alamy; 9(br) Trapper Frank/Corbis Sygma; 10, Digital Archive Japan/Alamy; 11, J.Riou/photocuisine/Corbis; 12, 24, Joshua Ets-Hokin/Corbis; 13, Michael Bradley/Staff/Getty; 14, The Anthony Blake Photo Library/Alamy; 16(tl), PSL Images/Alamy; 16(tr), 25, Christine Schneider/zefa/Corbis; 16(bl), Gary Houlder/Corbis; 16(br), Khaled Kassem/Alamy; 17, Bob Krist/Corbis; 18, Pitchal Frederic/Corbis; 19, Monnet Luc/Corbis Sygma; 20, Michael Busselle/Robert Harding World Imagery/Corbis; 21, 25, Phil Rees/Alamy; 22, Niall Benvie/Corbis; 23, Bubbles Photolibrary/Alamy

Contents

Words printed in **bold** can be found in the glossary.

What is packaging?

Packaging is everywhere. Almost everything we buy today comes in packaging. Packaging can be boxes, tins, bags, moulded plastic, bubble wrap, bottles or jars. It is used to protect, contain and present goods.

Packaging can stop things from breaking or being squashed by providing a hard shell or padding. It also keeps things clean and helps food to stay fresh for longer by keeping out dirt and **bacteria**.

FACT!

Nature packages things too! Our soft, delicate brains are packaged in hard, protective skulls. Snails' squashy bodies are protected by hard, strong shells.

Often things we buy have lots of parts or pieces, like a packet of biscuits or a board game. Packaging helps to keep all the separate bits together in one place and makes the **product** easy to **transport**.

Packaging looks good! **Manufacturers** make their products' packaging eye-catching so that we notice them and want to buy them.

◀ As a snail grows its shell grows too, so the snail always fits inside its protective packaging.

DVD boxes contain and protect the disc inside, while the pictures and information on the front aim to make a customer interested in the DVD itself. ▶

Packaging in history

Packaging has changed a lot since the barrels, jute sacks and wooden boxes which were used for storing and transporting goods over 300 years ago.

FACT!
The first packaging was used in prehistoric times! Animal parts and skins were used to hold water, and reeds were woven into baskets to hold food.

In the 1700s, simple paper labels began to appear on products, and hand-engraved designs could sometimes be found on tobacco wrappers and glove boxes. Even 100 years ago, people still bought most of their goods loose, and the required amount was weighed out and wrapped up in paper by shopkeepers.

Gradually, packaged goods became more common because it was easier to store and serve them than to weigh out and wrap loose food. Foods began to be sold in glass jars, paper packets, tins and cardboard boxes. Today, most foods are sold ready packaged.

◀ This shopkeeper is ladling milk from a canister into a jug for his customer to take home.

This packaging is from the 1920s. Are any of these products still on sale today? ▶

CEREALS
in
Sealed Packages

WHEAT
KRISPIES
FLAKES OF WHEAT
FLAVORED WITH MALT, SUGAR AND SALT

with the sweet
wheat flavor

NET WEIGHT
8 OUNCES

Kellogg's
RICE
KRISPIES
OVEN POPPED AND FLAVORED WITH MALT, SUGAR, SALT

snap crackle pop

Crisp
TO THE LAST SPOONFUL

MADE BY KELLOGG COMPANY, BATTLE CREEK, MICH.

Ladybug
Ladybug

Kellogg's
RICE KRISPIE

Butter

John

ROBERT A. JO

nston

aukee

arm
oda
ckers

Whole Grain Oats
Richest Thrifty
Natural Source
OF
VITAMIN B₁
(THIAMINE)

QUAKER

CK
QUA
KER
TS

3 LBS. NET

Company Address Chicago, U.S.A.

IGA
Quick Cook
ROLLED
OATS

CONTENTS 1 LB 4 OZ

QUIC

QUAKER
OATS

QUICK

QUAKER
OATS

WEIGHT 1 LB. 4 OZ. NET
The Quaker Oats Company

unshine
6½
-W. SODAS
From The
Thousand
Window
Bakeries
scuits

LES BISCUIT COMPANY
CHICAGO. ILL.
CHES IN OVER 100 CITIES

Sunshine Biscuits

Sunshine
SHREDDED
WHEAT
MADE ONLY FROM
100% WHOLE WHEAT
NOTHING ADDED

READY
TO SERVE

11 oz.
NET WEIGHT

12 TENDER
BISCUITS

KINGSFORD'S
CORN STARCH
EXPRESSLY FOR FOOD
MORE USES FROM
T. KINGSFORD & SON.

Corn Products Refining Co.

Pos
CEREAL

There's

POSTUM CEREAL

INSTANT
POSTUM
A BEVERAGE

Aunt Dinah
Brand
PURE
NEW ORLEANS
MOLASSES

ICK & FORD, LTD.

DELICACY, COMPOSED OF CORN SYRUP OF THE FINEST QUALITY
5 POUNDS NET WEIGHT

Karo

Corn Products Refining Co.

Penic
Syrup
CRYSTAL
WHITE
NET WEIGHT
5 POUNDS
NET CONTENTS
5 QT. 1 PT. 7 FL. OZ.

CORN SYRUP
RICH IN DEXTROSE
FOR PRESERVING - CANDY

PENICK & FORD
CEDAR RAPIDS, IOWA

Clover Farm
MADE IN U.S.A.

CLOVER FARM
STORES

GOLDEN TABLE
SYRUP
CONTENTS 5 LB.

Log
Cabin
Syrup

7

All kinds of packaging

Packaging today comes in all sorts of shapes and sizes, and is made from many materials. Different materials have different properties, which make them good for doing certain jobs.

Glass jars are used to contain sauces and jams. They don't let any air in until they are opened and they can be closed again after use.

Plastic bottles are used for all kinds of liquids. They are light and can easily be opened and closed again.

Plastic can be moulded to hold pies in place. This plastic is then put inside a box to protect the pies.

Boxes are used to contain all sorts of go They are strong and keep all the pieces product together.

Aluminium cans are designed to hold a single serving of a drink. They can't be closed again but they keep the fizz in fizzy drinks until they are opened.

Some items are packaged in cardboard boxes with a plastic window in the front. The box protects the product while the window lets the customer see inside.

These dolls are packaged in plastic bags so that they can be seen, but there is a cardboard tab at the top which gives information about the product.

Some products are sold in blister packaging. The plastic is moulded to fit the shape of the product and to hold it in place.

Packaging purposes

Packaging is designed to make sure a product reaches the customer in good condition. It keeps all the parts of the product together and makes it easy to sell. Different products need different types of packaging.

Toys are made in many different countries and are shipped across the world. Their packaging is designed to protect them and to stop any small pieces from getting lost. The packaging must also be easy to transport and **attractive** to buyers.

Ready-meals are sold in plastic trays with clear film stretched over the top. The tray must be made of a special plastic that will not melt in a hot oven. The film lets the buyer see the product inside and can be pierced to let steam escape from the hot food while it is cooking.

All this is presented in a cardboard box which shows information, looks good, and makes the product easy to store and move around.

◀ The packaging on ready-meals makes them quick and easy to cook.

Egg boxes are made of a thick cardboard and are specially shaped to protect the eggs inside. ▶

Looking good!

Manufacturers know that the product they make has to compete with other, similar products in the shops. That is why they think very hard about making packaging look good. If they develop a particular style and a logo, people can easily recognise a product they enjoyed, and buy it again and again.

A product is usually made for a particular group of people. The packaging needs to **appeal** to the group the product is made for, so that those people will want to buy it. Manufacturers spend a lot of money on developing attractive packaging so that people will buy the product it contains.

Packaging for children needs to be bright, fun and eye-catching, so that children want to buy it. Children's chocolates look very different from a box of luxury chocolates. The packaging for luxury chocolates often looks expensive and grown-up, so that adults feel they are buying a special treat.

Do you think these chocolates were made for adults or for children?

Try it out!

DESIGN THE LOOK OF THE PACKAGING FOR A NEW BATH PRODUCT

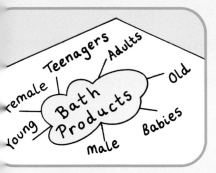

Think about what group of people might enjoy your product.

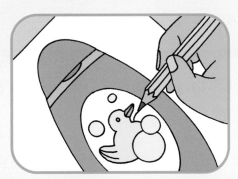

2 Sketch your design on paper, or use a graphics program on a computer.

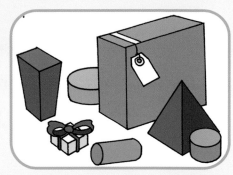

3 Think about the effect the shape and size of the package and the colours you choose will create.

Experiment with different sizes and styles of lettering. If you are using a computer, try out different **fonts**.

What kind of person do you think this Easter egg was designed for? ▶

Making boxes

Cardboard boxes are the most common type of packaging. They are strong but not heavy, and they can be padded inside to keep their contents safe. Cuboid-shaped boxes are easy to stack and store. They fit together without any gaps, so they don't waste any space.

Even though cardboard boxes come in many shapes and sizes, they are nearly all made in the same way. They are created from a template called a **net**. Machines in factories cut and **score** sheets of cardboard to make box nets. Other machines fold up the sides and fix them in place with tape or glue.

Folding cardboard makes it into a strong **structure**. Some boxes are made even stronger by using thicker or **corrugated** cardboard, or by fixing the sides and corners with staples. Boxes used for **transit** need to be very strong to stop goods from getting crushed on their journey.

Cardboard boxes can be big enough to hold televisions and washing machines, or small enough to hold sweets and popcorn.

Try it out!
MAKE A BOX FROM YOUR OWN NET

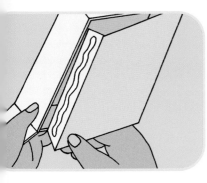

Take a box apart carefully along the seams. A cereal box is a good choice.

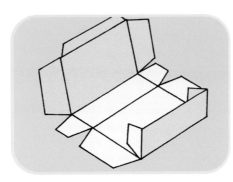

2 Can you see how the box has been made? Are there any flaps or tabs to make the box easier to stick together? Has the box been stiffened or strengthened in any way?

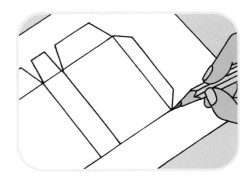

3 Make a sketch of the net of your box. Which lengths are the same? Why do you think this is?

4 Nets can be used to make lots of different shaped boxes. Can you work out how to draw a net that would make a long, triangle-shaped box?

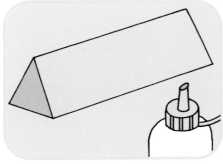

5 Try folding your net up and see if it works. If not, think about what changes you need to make to your net to make it work.

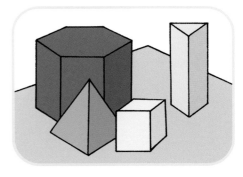

6 Once you have a net that works, stick it together with glue or sticky tape.

Bags of fun!

Bags are used to package all sorts of things and can be made from many different materials. They are a very common type of packaging because they are simple to make and very easy to carry. Most bags are made by machines in factories.

▲ Plastic bags are used for carrying shopping as they are very light but quite strong.

▲ Cellophane is a kind of plastic that can keep things fresh. Sweets are often sold in cellophane bags.

▲ Paper bags are cheap to make but don't keep things fresh. Fruit and veg that don't have their own packaging are often carried in paper bags.

▲ Crisps and snacks are sold in foil bags because they are good for keeping things fresh too.

Try it out!
YOU CAN MAKE YOUR OWN PAPER BAGS
You will need: **a large sheet of paper (newspaper is fine) and tape**

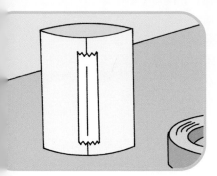

Make the paper into a cylinder and tape the overlap. Fold the cylinder flat.

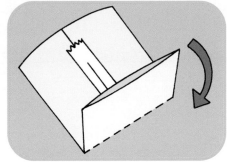

2 Make a fold about a third of the way up from the bottom. Crease it sharply and unfold it again.

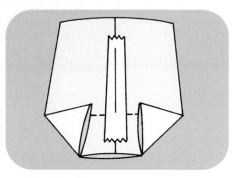

3 At each end of the crease, fold the corners in to meet the fold.

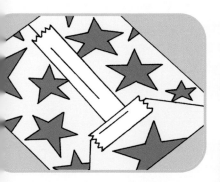

Now tape the bottom of the bag shut. When it is dry, decorate your bag!

This machine makes plastic carrier bags. ▶

Moulding materials

Some materials can be made into different shapes using moulds. Moulding is used to make all kinds of different packaging.

When plastic, metal and glass are heated at very high temperatures they become soft and can be moulded to make cans, jars, trays, bottles and bottle tops.

Drinks are often sold in packaging which has been made from a mould. Moulded bottles and cans are **water-tight** and less likely to leak.

Toys are sometimes packaged in plastic which has been moulded to fit the shape of the product exactly. The plastic is clear so that people can see the toy inside, and the toy is held in place by the moulded shape. This kind of packaging is called a blister pack.

◄ Glass is poured into these moulds to make bottles for wine.

Try it out!
INVESTIGATE PACKAGING FOR DRINKS

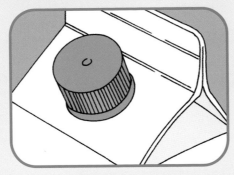

Look at a range of drink containers. What are the containers made from? What makes them water-tight? Why has the manufacturer chosen each material? Have they all been moulded, or have some been made in other ways?

2 Have the drinks been packaged to be drunk all in one go, or can they be re-closed and finished another time? How do you think this affects the design of the packaging?

What material do you think makes the best packaging for drinks? Have a go at designing your own drinks packaging and label each of its features.

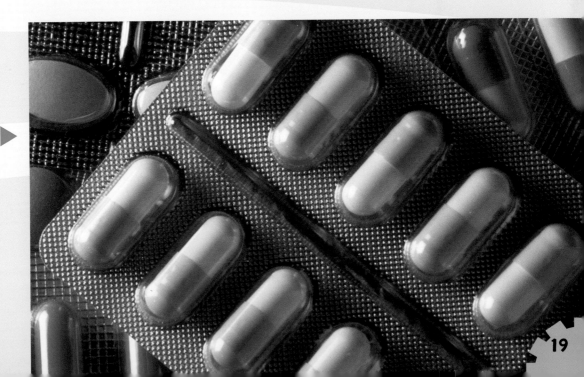

ablets are often ackaged in moulded lastic so that each ne is kept separate. oil is stuck onto the back so the tablets an be popped out ne at a time.

What a waste!

Some products are sold with a lot of packaging to keep them safe or fresh, while other products need very little packaging at all.

Hard fruits like oranges don't need a lot of packaging as they have thick skins to protect the soft flesh inside. They are sold loose or in a net bag. Soft fruits like raspberries need more packaging, and come in plastic or waxed board cartons with bubble wrap at the bottom, to protect the fruit.

Toys like balls or skipping ropes are sold with very little packaging or none at all. Magic sets or model making kits have lots of separate parts, so they have more packaging to keep all the pieces together.

Packaging can be expensive to make. It is usually thrown away once the product is opened and ends up as waste, so it is good to use as little packaging as possible.

◀ Fruit is displayed without packaging on this fruit stall.

Try it out!

DESIGN AND MAKE PACKAGING FOR SIX STRAWBERRIES

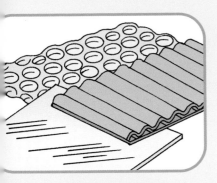  

Design packaging that will keep six strawberries from being squashed or bruised, as well as keeping them clean and fresh. Use as little packaging as possible to achieve this. What materials will you use? How will the packaging protect the contents? Will it open and shut? Will you be able to see your fruit?

2 Sketch out your design. Look at your design carefully and think about it. Show a friend and ask them to **evaluate** your ideas. Is there anything you could do to make it better?

3 Make your packaging and test it out. Put your strawberries in the packaging, and move them around several times. Don't be too delicate – you want it to be a real test! Are your strawberries safe? Could you have used less packaging?

Two pairs of these biking gloves are packaged in cellophane bags while two are packaged with a small card label. Which packaging do you think is the best to use? Can you think of a better way to package gloves?

Reduce, reuse and recycle

Packaging makes up a huge part of the rubbish we throw away. Most of this is food and drink packaging.

Our rubbish is buried in big holes in the ground called **landfill sites**. Landfill sites take up a huge amount of space and are bad for our **environment**. We should try not to throw away too much packaging, and look for products with packaging that is environmentally friendly.

Packaging can often be reused or made into something else. Ice-cream tubs and plastic bags can be saved and used again. Lots of materials can be **recycled**. Plastic, metal and glass can be melted down and made into something new. Paper and cardboard can be made into toilet paper, newspaper or even greeting cards!

FACT!
Packaging often becomes litter in our local area. Litter spoils our environment and harms wildlife, so packaging should always be disposed of properly.

◀ There are about 4000 licensed landfill sites in the UK.

Try it out!

DO YOUR BEST TO REDUCE, REUSE AND RECYCLE

1 Think about how you can reduce the amount of packaging you throw away. You could carry your drink in a reusable bottle, instead of using a new carton every day. Or take an apple for lunch instead of a packet of crisps so that you would have no packet to throw away.

2 Before you throw any packaging away, think about whether you might be able to reuse it. Could you decorate your empty shoebox and keep special things in it?

3 Start a recycling bank at home or in your classroom. Find out which materials can be recycled, and see how much of your empty packaging can be put to good use.

Recycling banks can be found in all towns and cities. In some areas recycling is collected by the local council. ▶

Make your own...

DESIGN AND MAKE YOUR OWN BISCUIT PACKAGING

Design a biscuit package that will hold four biscuits and will protect them from breaking when they are dropped from a height of 1.5 metres onto the floor.

Think about what your packaging needs to do and who it is aimed at. Are your biscuits for children or adults? How will this affect your final design? What materials will you use to make your packaging? What properties will it need to have?

Sketch your packaging and add notes to your drawing to remind you of good ideas. Show your sketch to a friend. Tell them about the features of your packaging. Be prepared to do some more thinking if your friend thinks of possible problems.

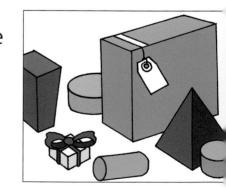

Make a mock-up of your design with paper. This should give you an idea of how well your packaging is going to work. When you are satisfied with your design, start making your packaging. Be prepared to stop at any point and think 'This needs to change.' It can sometimes take time to get a design just right.

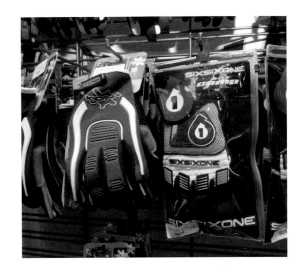

Test your biscuit package! Measure 1.5 metres, and drop the package. Are the biscuits still whole inside?

Evaluate your work. Show a group of friends your finished package and explain why it is suitable for your biscuits. How well does the package protect the biscuits? What makes it attractive? Will your biscuits stay fresh? Is there anything you would do differently next time to make it work better?

Brilliant books and wonderful websites

There are lots of great books and websites out there to help you to learn more about packaging. When you are using the Internet, remember to be careful. Do not give out details of your age or where you live, and make sure your parents and carers have a look at the websites you are visiting. They may learn something too!

BOOKS

The Way Things Work by David Macaulay and Neil Ardley (Dorling Kindersley, 2004)

Dotty Inventions: And Some Real Ones Too by Roger McGough (Frances Lincoln, 2005)

The Oxford Children's A-Z of Technology by Robin Kerrod (OUP, 2004)

Where Does Rubbish Go? by S. Tahta (Usborne, 2001)

Why Should I Recycle? by Jen Green (Hodder Wayland, 2002)

Bug Boxes by Julia Warin (St Martins Press, 1994)

WEBSITES

www.epa.gov/recyclecity/market
Recycle City

www.epa.gov/epaoswer/osw/kids/quest
Exciting activities about 'Nature's packaging'

www.wasteonline.org.uk
Waste Watch – all about rubbish and recycling

www.eco-schools.org.uk
Eco Schools – lots of information about waste, with fun activities

www.southampton.gov.uk/environment/rubbish-collections/schools
Ideas for schools about reducing waste

www.cadburylearningzone.co.uk/maths/learningzone/chocolatechallenge
Design and make your own chocolate bar and packaging online

Glossary

appeal	attract the interest of someone
attractive	pleasing
bacteria	tiny living things which live all over the Earth and in the bodies of people and animals
contents	what something contains
corrugated	material shaped into even ridges or grooves
cuboid	a 3-D shape with six rectangular sides
environment	the world around you
evaluate	judge what you have done and decide if anything could be done better
fonts	different styles of type
jute	a strong, coarse fibre made from certain plants
landfill sites	a low area of land that is filled with rubbish
manufacturers	a person, group or company that makes a product
net	a template which you can fold up to make a box
product	something that has been made
properties	the qualities or characteristics of something
recycle	to make a material ready to use again
score	make a mark or a scratch on something so that it can be easily bent
structure	something that has been built
transit	moving something from one place to another
transport	to move something from one place to another
water-tight	won't let any liquid through

Index

Numbers in **bold** denote a picture.